I0606186

My Pet Hawk

Note: Removing a baby bird from its nest could harm the bird. If you find an injured or abandoned baby bird, talk to your parents or a local wildlife officer.

The Nunavummi reading series is a Nunavut-developed levelled book series that supports literacy development while teaching readers about the people, traditions, and environment of the Canadian Arctic.

Published in Canada by Nunavummi, an imprint of Inhabit Education Books Inc. | www.inhabiteducationbooks.com

Inhabit Education Books Inc.
(Iqaluit) P.O. Box 2129, Iqaluit, Nunavut, X0A 1H0
(Toronto) 614 Mount Pleasant Road, Unit 1, Toronto, Ontario, M4S 2M8

Printed in Canada.

Library and Archives Canada Cataloguing in Publication

Title: My pet hawk / written by Etua Snowball ; illustrated by Erin Hunting.
Names: Snowball, Etua, 1972- author. | Hunting, Erin, illustrator.
Series: Nunavummi reading series.
Description: Series statement: Nunavummi reading series
Identifiers: Canadiana 20230131085 | ISBN 9781774506066 (hardcover)
Subjects: LCGFT: Picture books. | LCGFT: Fiction.
Classification: LCC PS8637.N75 M9 2023 | DDC jC813/.6—dc23

ISBN: 978-1-77450-606-6

This project has been made possible in part by the Government of Canada.

My Pet Hawk

WRITTEN BY
Etua Snowball
ILLUSTRATED BY
Erin Hunting

I am going to tell you a story from when I was a teenager. We were staying at our summer cabin, and something happened that I will never forget.

It started one day when I kept sensing that something was looking at me from high above. I gazed up. There was a dot in the sky that didn't seem to move. It stayed beside a cloud right above me.

I watched the dot closely. Then, it suddenly moved down. I saw that it was a hawk. When it came close to the ground, it swooped and went right back up. It was holding onto what looked like a lemming.

It was amazing to see the hawk catch an animal so easily. I wasn't paying attention to the people around me anymore. I just watched where the hawk was headed. I assumed it had a nest.

I saw the hawk fly far away and land on a cliff on the other side of the falls.

I thought about the hawk a lot after that day. I decided that the next time we went fishing on the other side of the falls, I would look for the nest. I had always wanted a pet that flew.

My family had a business taking tourists out fishing. We usually went fishing on the ocean, but sometimes we went to the falls.

One day, the weather was too windy to go fishing on the ocean. Instead, we planned to go fishing near the falls. I knew this would be my opportunity to find the nest.

That morning, I accidentally slept in late. I missed the boats leaving for the falls. There was a way to get there by foot, so I decided to walk. I quickly got dressed, ate breakfast, and headed out the door.

The walk was long, but I finally arrived. I saw lots of tourists fishing by the river. I looked up at the big cliff where I had seen the hawk go. I knew that was where its nest must be. On the other side of the cliff, the slope was not as steep. That's where I could climb up.

I needed to get across the river to reach the cliff. I waited until a tourist wanted to go across so I could go on their boat. Finally, I saw a man who wanted to cross. I waved for a guide to come over with a canoe to take us.

When we got across the river, I grabbed a rope from the boat. Then I started walking up the hill.

It was windy but hot, and I soon started sweating. I took off my jacket and planned to pick it up on the way back.

Finally, I made it to the top. I tried to look down the cliffside, but it was scary to be so high up. I took a deep breath and looked over the edge.

I saw a white area on the side of the cliff. It looked like bird poop. *That must be where the nest is*, I thought.

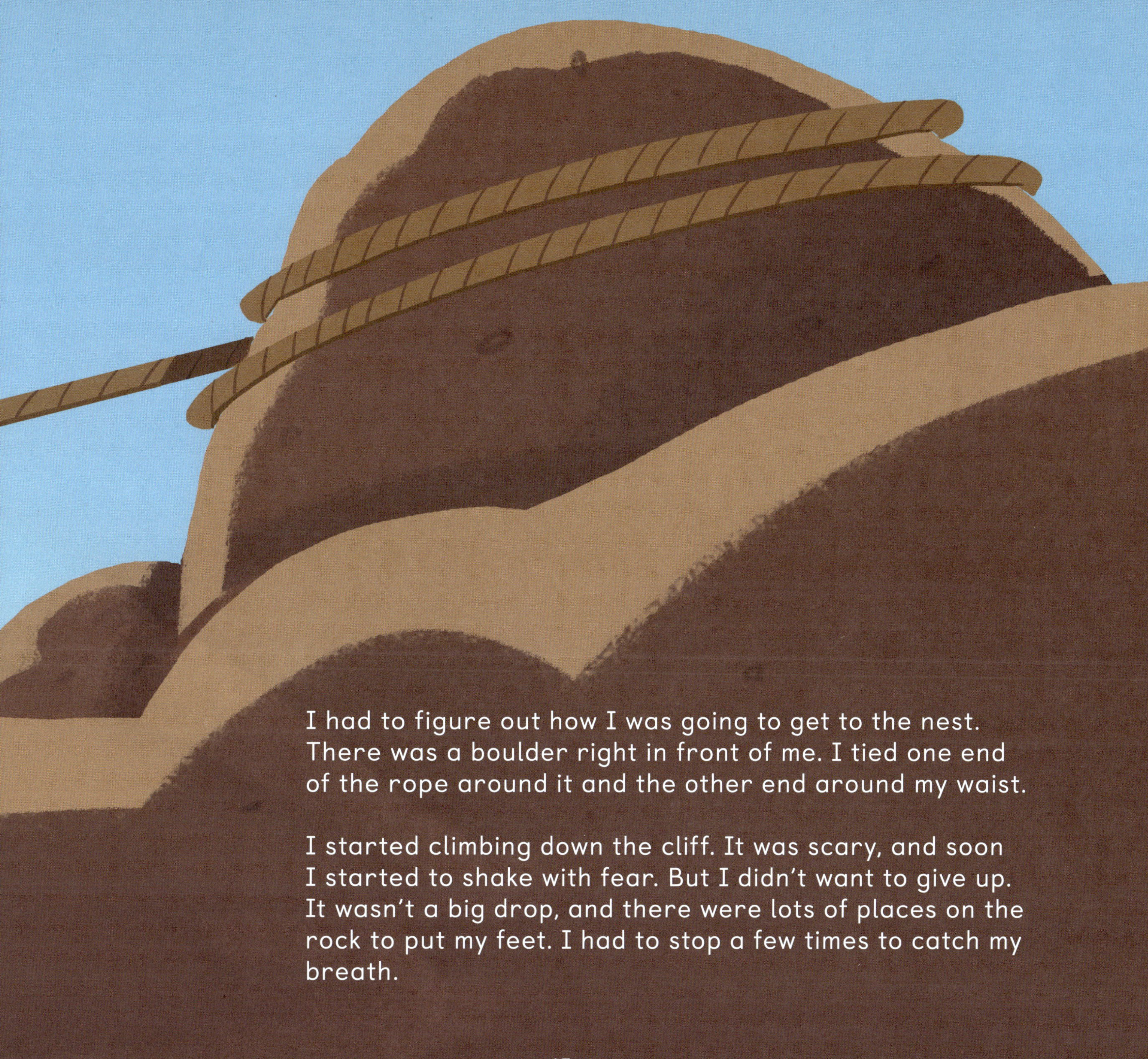

I had to figure out how I was going to get to the nest. There was a boulder right in front of me. I tied one end of the rope around it and the other end around my waist.

I started climbing down the cliff. It was scary, and soon I started to shake with fear. But I didn't want to give up. It wasn't a big drop, and there were lots of places on the rock to put my feet. I had to stop a few times to catch my breath.

Finally, I got close enough to see the baby hawks in their nest. They had down-like fur in beautiful shades of gold and brown. They just stared at me. They had probably never seen anything like me before.

There were three babies of different sizes. I chose the biggest one to be my pet. I thought it would be able to fly sooner. When I tried to pick it up, it started biting me. But eventually it stopped fighting and let me take it. Maybe it was in shock.

I held the hawk in my right arm and started climbing back up the cliff with my left. It seemed a lot faster going up than down, maybe because of my excitement. When I got to the top, I put the hawk in a soft spot as I wound up the rope.

When I went to pick up the hawk again, it faced me with its mouth wide open. It looked like it was going to bite me again. I nervously picked it up by its back and started walking. I felt very proud of myself for successfully completing my journey. I couldn't stop smiling as I walked back.

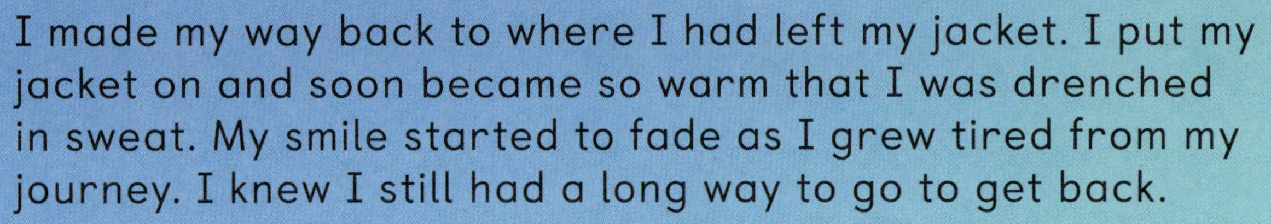

I made my way back to where I had left my jacket. I put my jacket on and soon became so warm that I was drenched in sweat. My smile started to fade as I grew tired from my journey. I knew I still had a long way to go to get back.

I met up with the tourist and the guide again to go back across the river. The tourist saw that I was holding the hawk and said how beautiful it was. The guide looked annoyed that I had taken so long.

When I finally got home, I was exhausted. I laid some grass in a box and put the baby hawk in it. I left the box outside our cabin for the night.

When I woke up the next day, I didn't go fishing with the group. I quickly went to see how the baby hawk was doing.

I looked in the box and saw its big eyes staring at me. It seemed hungry, so I got some fish. I didn't know if hawks ate fish, but that was the only thing I had ready.

It ate the fish quickly, so I kept feeding it.

After eating a lot of fish, the hawk started vomiting. I thought maybe it had eaten too fast. I kept feeding it fish, but it always vomited it up. It didn't seem well, so I realized that it probably didn't eat fish. I needed to find something else for it to eat.

Then I remembered that I had seen its mother hunting lemmings when I first saw it.

I quickly went looking for lemmings. I looked and looked, but I couldn't find any. It was starting to seem hopeless.

As I walked home, I felt sad that I couldn't give the hawk what it needed. Suddenly, a lemming popped up right in front of me. I chased it, but it was moving quickly and turning in different directions. Finally, I saw that it was going to turn left, and I got there first and stepped on it.

I proudly returned to the baby hawk with the lemming in my hand. The hawk opened its mouth as soon as it saw what I was holding. It quickly swallowed the lemming and looked eager for more. *How am I going to get more lemmings?* I thought.

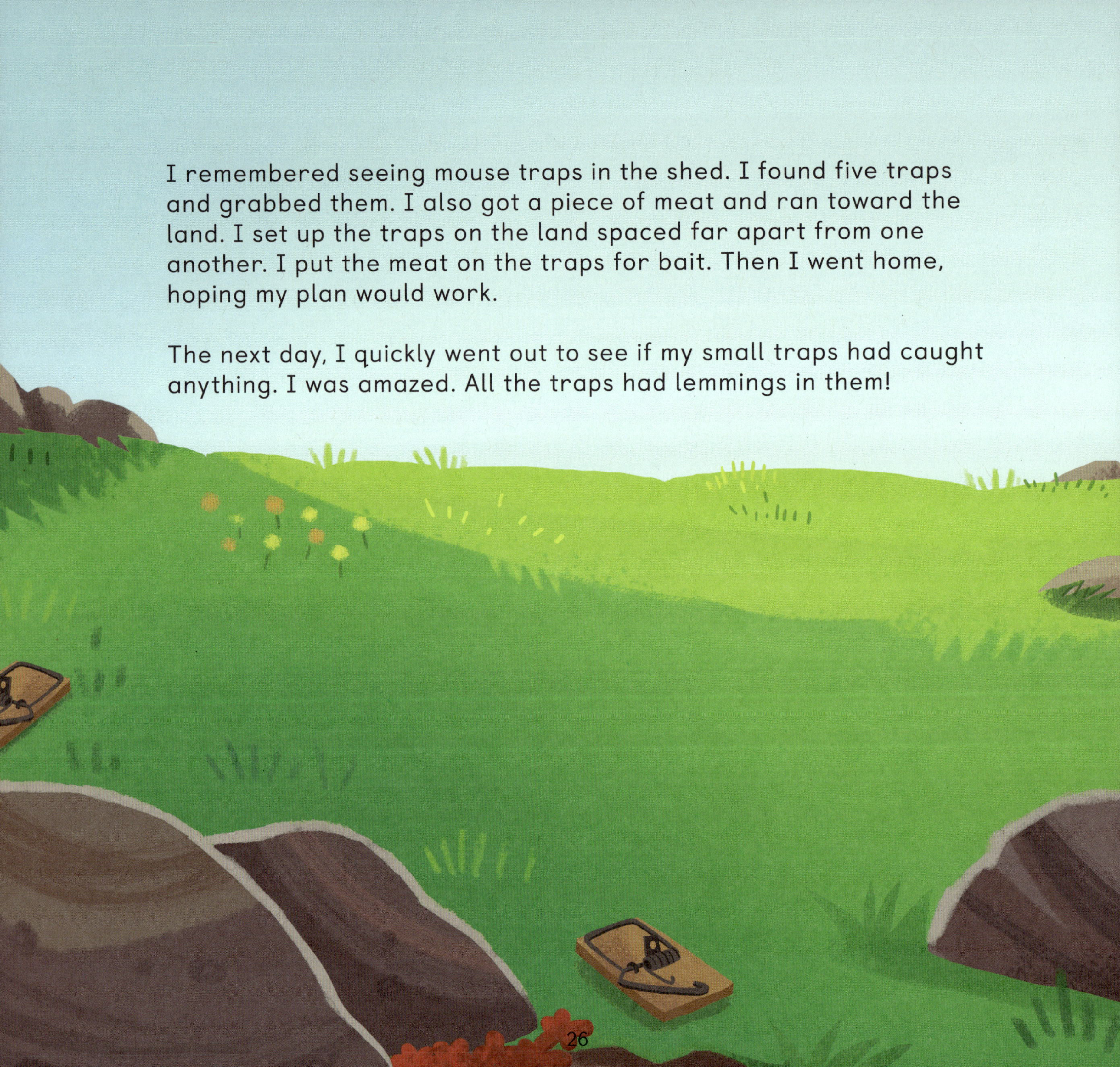

I remembered seeing mouse traps in the shed. I found five traps and grabbed them. I also got a piece of meat and ran toward the land. I set up the traps on the land spaced far apart from one another. I put the meat on the traps for bait. Then I went home, hoping my plan would work.

The next day, I quickly went out to see if my small traps had caught anything. I was amazed. All the traps had lemmings in them!

I collected lemmings this way for a while. I fed the hawk in the morning and at the end of the day when we returned from fishing. The hawk was growing bigger and stronger. I made it a little fence enclosure outside the cabin. Soon it started walking toward me when it saw me coming.

As it grew, it lost its fluffy down feathers. It started to move its wings more, but it still didn't fly.

I let the hawk follow me when I went to check the lemming traps. It walked and hopped, trailing behind me. It had learned that it was going to eat when we went for walks. It also knew exactly where to go.

I realized that the hawk wouldn't be able to hunt animals if it always ate dead things. I decided I needed to teach it to hunt. But it would be hard because we never saw any live lemmings when we went looking for them. I would need to get creative.

I had a lot of dead lemmings from the traps, so I tied one to a long piece of string. On the other end, I made a handle from a branch. Then I went to check my lemming traps. As usual, the young hawk followed along. Little did it know, it was going to get a hunting lesson.

I started dragging the dead lemming behind me. Then I started running. The hawk chased it with its wings open. It couldn't catch up to me, so I slowed down. I wanted the hawk to catch it. Then the hawk grabbed the lemming and started eating it.

After that, we practised hunting every day. The hawk started flying short distances. It also started to get faster.

The hawk always stayed on my wrist when it wanted to be with me. Sometimes when I got tired, it moved to my shoulder.

One day, I arrived home from taking tourists fishing in the late afternoon. I was exhausted, but I took the hawk to practise hunting. The hawk flew and caught the dead lemming in an instant! Then it went right to my wrist after swallowing it. I was proud that the hawk was becoming a strong hunter.

The next day, when I got home I grabbed a dead lemming and started walking as usual. But I noticed the hawk was not following me. When I tried to give it the dead lemming, the hawk didn't want it. It flew directly up, high in the sky. It seemed like it was showing me what it could do.

I realized that the hawk didn't need to be fed anymore. It could hunt on its own. I decided to go get the lemming traps so I wouldn't kill off what the hawk could hunt for itself.

38

Every day when I walked toward the cabin, the hawk would come to land on my wrist. It didn't need anything from me except my company. Sometimes it would fly away to where I couldn't see it, but it always came back.

One day when I got home, the hawk didn't come to me. I couldn't see it anywhere, and I was worried it got hurt. Later that evening, I heard the hawk making noises outside. I quickly went outside to see it. The hawk walked right toward me holding a dead lemming in its beak. It had lost me and wanted to show me what it caught.

Another day, I came home and again the hawk didn't show up. I didn't hear it all evening. I was worried but decided to go to bed. I was exhausted from taking tourists out all day.

The next morning, I still didn't see it. When I got home later in the day, it suddenly came to land on my wrist, startling me. I put my arm out to look at it and make sure it wasn't hurt. I could see that the hawk was fine. I could feel its wisdom and knew that it would be on its own soon. It would no longer greet me.

The hawk flew away, and I watched it head toward the cliff where I had first seen it. It had likely found its family there.

The hawk didn't show up for many days after that. I was not worried anymore, knowing that it was able to take care of itself and was likely with its family. It did still come once in a while, but it kept its distance and landed on a boulder instead of on me. I missed it, but I had to accept that it was better off on its own.

Eventually the hawk stopped showing up at all. But I still felt it watching me from high above. I only ever saw it high in the sky. It never came close again.

I missed my pet hawk, but I was grateful that I had a friend that was completely different from me. When it came time for my family to go to Kuujjuaq for the winter, I kept looking up to see if I could see the hawk. I never saw it again.

Nunavummi

Nunavummi
Reading Series

The Nunavummi reading series is a Nunavut-developed levelled book series that supports literacy development while teaching readers about the people, traditions, and environment of the Canadian Arctic.

- 24–40 pages
- Sentences are complex and vary in length
- Lots of varied punctuation
- Dialogue is included in fiction texts and is necessary to understand the story
- Readers rely on the words to decode the text; images are present but only somewhat supportive

- 24–56 pages
- Sentences can be more complicated and are not always restricted to a structure that readers are familiar with
- Some unfamiliar themes and genres are introduced
- Readers rely on the words to decode the text; images are present but only somewhat supportive

- 24–64 pages
- Chapter books introduced
- Readers may be exposed to new genres (science fiction, mysteries, biographies, etc.) and unfamiliar themes and settings
- Illustrations are somewhat supportive and may not be included on every spread of pages

Fountas & Pinnell Text Level: N

This book has been officially levelled using the F&P Text Level Gradient™ Leveling System.